Born Slaves

Born Slaves

An easier-to-read and abridged version of
the classic "The Bondage of the Will" by
Martin Luther, first published
in 1525.

Prepared by Clifford Pond

Joint Managing Editors
J.P. Arthur M.A.
H.J. Appleby

GRACE PUBLICATIONS TRUST
139 Grosvenor Avenue
London N5 2NH
England

First published 1984
Second impression 1994
Third impression 1998
Fourth impression 2008

ISBN 978 0 946462 02 5

Distributed by: EVANGELICAL PRESS
Grange Close
Faverdale North
Darlington DL3 0PH
England

Printed in Great Britain by: CPI Cox & Wyman,
Reading, RG1 8EX

Cover design: L. L. Evans

Contents:

(The material in this book which is an abridgement of Luther's work is found in Chapters one to four. The Preface, Introduction and Postscript are present-day comments on Luther's work. Ed.)

Preface:

The question.

The question is — does man have something called 'free-will'? Can a man freely and without help turn to Christ for salvation from his sins? Erasmus answers: 'Yes!' Luther says a resounding: 'No!' Luther was convinced that 'free-will' strikes at the heart of the biblical doctrine of salvation by grace alone, through faith alone. We must have the same conviction. We must fight against 'free-will' as vigorously as Luther did. Erasmus said: 'I can conceive of "free-will" as a power of human will by which a man may apply himself to those things that lead to eternal salvation or turn away from them'. To this we also must give a resolute 'No! Man is born a slave to sin!' He is not free.

Introduction:

The background to the book and the controversy with Erasmus.

Martin Luther wrote THE BONDAGE OF THE WILL in answer to the teaching of Desiderius Erasmus who was born in Rotterdam between 1466 and 1469. Erasmus was an augustinian monk for seven years and then he travelled to England. There he met men who made him eager to pursue his study of Greek. Eventually Erasmus produced a critical text of the Greek New Testament (1516). He rejected fanciful methods of interpreting the scriptures and many of the superstitions of church teachers. He rebelled against the laziness and vice common in the monasteries. But despite this, Erasmus was not an evangelical believer. He was a humanist, believing that men could earn their salvation instead of relying only on Jesus Christ, his death and resurrection. Erasmus rightly preferred a simple approach to christian teaching, rather than the complicated hair-splitting of the professional theologians. He avoided controversy and for a long time did not come into the open on the issue of 'free-will', but when he did, it was a challenge that Martin Luther could not ignore.

Martin Luther was born in Saxony and was about fourteen years younger than Erasmus. While Luther was a monk, he had a dramatic experience of the gospel of God's grace. From that time he knew that

9

every experience and belief must be tested by the authority of scripture. He knew that salvation is by 'grace through faith and this not from yourselves, it is the gift of God — not of works, so that no-one can boast' (Ephesians 2:8—9). His own experience confirmed that conviction.

Luther was a professor, a theologian and also a pastor. His people knew he felt what he preached. He was no dry scholar. He felt the pressure of eternity every time he preached. This compelled him sometimes to do unpopular and even dangerous things. He was prepared to stand for God's truth against the whole world.

At first, Erasmus appeared to be on Luther's side because both men rejected many of the errors and failings of the Roman church. But Luther challenged, more and more, the Roman teaching of salvation by works, insisting that 'the just shall live by faith' (Romans 1:17). Erasmus was still in the Roman church and as a scholar he at last yielded to his church's pressure to state the teaching of 'free-will'. In defiance of Luther's request to him not to do so, he issued his DISCUSSION CONCERNING 'FREE-WILL' in 1524. Erasmus wrote to Henry VIII: 'The die is cast. The little book on "free-will" has seen the light of day'. The book pleased the Pope and the Roman Emperor and was praised by Henry VIII.

Luther now declared Erasmus to be an enemy of the evangelical faith. God over-ruled the intense quarrel between these two men to the advantage of his kingdom. It produced a great statement of evangelical doctrine that has enriched Christ's church ever since — Luther's BONDAGE OF THE WILL. We offer here a summary of this great work. We have retained much of Luther's style but have not followed Luther's order.

We begin where Luther left off, by first summarising his positive doctrine of the bondage of the will. We follow this with other sections in which Luther states, and then refutes, Erasmus' arguments.

Luther's style would normally cause us to add certain words every time he uses the expression 'free-will'. For example: the free-will *that you suppose exists*. But we have chosen to reflect Luther's meaning by using quotation marks — 'free-will'. And in chapters two, three and four, we have retained Luther's direct speech, keeping as closely as possible to the atmosphere of his work.

We have not included every argument Luther uses because to do so would enlarge this simplification unduly.

Chapter One

What the scriptures teach.

The scriptures are like several armies opposed to the idea that man has a 'free-will' to choose and receive salvation. But it will be enough for me to bring two generals into the fight — Paul and John, with a few of their forces.

Argument 1: The universal guilt of mankind proves 'free-will' to be false

In Romans 1:18 Paul teaches that all men without exception deserve to be punished by God. 'The wrath of God is being revealed from heaven against all the godlessness and wickedness of men who suppress the truth by their wickedness'. If all men have 'free-will' and yet all without exception are under God's wrath, then it follows that 'free-will' leads them in only one direction — 'godlessness and wickedness'. So where is the power of 'free-will' helping them to do good? If 'free-will' exists, it doesn't seem to be able to help men to salvation because it still leaves them under the wrath of God.

But some people accuse me of not following Paul closely enough. They claim that Paul's words 'against all the godlessness and wickedness of men who suppress

the truth by their wickedness' do not mean that everyone without exception is guilty in God's sight. They
argue that the text leaves it possible that some people
do not 'suppress the truth by their wickedness'. But
Paul is using a Hebrew form of words which leaves no
doubt that he means the wickedness of all men.

Furthermore, notice what Paul wrote just before it.
In verse 16 Paul declares the gospel to be 'the power of
God for the salvation of everyone who believes'. This
must mean that apart from the power of God in the
gospel, no-one has strength on his own to turn to God.
Paul goes on to say that this applies both to the Jews
and to the Greeks. The Jews knew the laws of God in
minute detail but this did not save them from God's
wrath. The Greeks enjoyed wonderful cultural benefits
but these brought them no nearer to God. There were
Jews and Greeks who tried hard to make themselves
right with God. But in spite of all their advantages
and their 'free-will', they failed completely. Paul does
not hesitate to condemn them all.

Then notice that in verse 17 Paul says that
'a righteousness from God is revealed'. So God shows
his righteousness to men. But God is not foolish. If men
did not need God's help, he would not waste his time
giving it to them. Every time people are converted it is
because God has come to them and overcome their
ignorance by showing the gospel to them. Without this,
they could never save themselves. No-one in all human
history has thought out by himself the fact of God's
wrath as it is taught in scripture. No-one ever dreamed
of getting peace with God through the life and work of
a unique Saviour, the God-Man, Jesus Christ. In fact the
Jews rejected Christ in spite of all the teaching of their
prophets. It seems that the very goodness that some
Jews and Gentiles reached, stopped them seeking God

in his way because they were determined to do things in their own way. So, the more 'free-will' tries, the worse things become.

There isn't a third group of people somewhere in between believers and unbelievers — a group capable of saving themselves. Jews and Gentiles make up the whole of mankind and they are all under God's wrath. None has the ability to turn to God. He must show himself to them first. If it were possible by 'free-will' to discover the truth, surely one Jew somewhere would have done so! The very highest reasonings of the Gentiles and the very strongest efforts of the best of the Jews (Romans 1:21; 2:23,28 and 29) did not bring them anywhere near to faith in Christ. They were condemned sinners along with all the rest. If all men have a 'free-will' and all men are guilty and condemned, then this supposed 'free-will' is powerless to bring them to faith in Christ. So, their will is not free after all.

Argument 2: The universal rule of sin proves 'free-will' to be false

We must let Paul explain his own teaching. In Romans 3:9 he says: 'What shall we conclude then? Are we (Jews) any better (than the Gentiles)? Not at all! We have already made the charge that Jews and Gentiles alike are all under sin'.

Not only are all men without exception declared to be guilty in God's sight, they are slaves to the sin that makes them guilty. This includes the Jews who thought they were not slaves of sin because they had the law of God. Since neither Jews nor Gentiles have been able to rid themselves of this slavery, there is obviously no power in man to help him to do good.

17

This universal slavery to sin includes those who appear to be the best and most upright. No matter how much goodness men may naturally achieve, this is not the same thing as the knowledge of God. The most excellent thing about men is their reason and their will but it has to be acknowledged that this noblest part is corrupt. Paul says in Romans 3:10—12: 'As it is written, "There is no-one righteous, not even one; there is no-one who understands, no-one who seeks God. All have turned away, they have together become worthless; there is no-one who does good, not even one".' The meaning of these words is perfectly clear. It is in the reason and the will that God is known. But no-one by nature knows God. We must conclude therefore that man's will is corrupt and man is totally unable by himself to know God or to please him.

Perhaps some brave individual will say that we are able to do more than we actually perform. But we are concerned here with what we are able to do, not with what we may or may not actually do. The scriptures quoted by Paul in Romans 3:10—12 will not allow us to make such a distinction. God condemns both the sinful inability of men as well as their corrupt acts. If men were able in the slightest degree to try to move in God's direction, there would be no need for God to save them. He would allow them to save themselves. But no man is able even to attempt it.

In Romans 3:19 Paul declares that every mouth is to be shut tight because no-one may argue against God's judgment of them for there is nothing in anyone that God can praise — not even a will that is free to turn to him. If someone says: 'I do have a little ability of my own to turn to God', that must mean he thinks there is something in him that God must praise and not condemn. His mouth is not shut! But this contradicts scripture.

God has said that *all* mouths are shut. It isn't just certain groups of people who are guilty before God. It isn't just the Pharisees among the Jews who are condemned. If this were so, then the remaining Jews would have had some power of their own to keep the law and avoid being guilty. But even the best of men are condemned for their ungodliness. They are spiritually dead in the same way as those who do not try to keep God's law at all. All men are ungodly and guilty, deserving to be punished by God. These things are so clear that no-one can whisper a word against them!

Argument 3: 'Free-will' is not able to gain acceptance with God through keeping the moral and ceremonial law

I argue that when Paul says in Romans 3:20—21: 'No-one will be declared righteous in God's sight by observing the law', he means the moral law (the ten commandments) as well as the ceremonial law. An idea has spread abroad that Paul means only the ceremonial law — the ritual of animal sacrifices, and temple worship. It is extraordinary that men have called Jerome who invented this idea a saint! I would call him something else! Jerome said that the death of Christ ended any possibility of being justified (declared righteous) by keeping the ceremonial law. But he left entirely open the possibility of being justified by keeping the moral law in our own strength, without God's help.

My answer is that if Paul only meant the ceremonial law, his argument is meaningless. Paul is contending that all men are unrighteous and in need of God's special grace — the love, wisdom and power of God by which he saves us. The result of Jerome's idea would be that God's grace is needed to save us from ceremonial law but not from the moral law. But we cannot keep the moral law, apart from grace. You can scare people into keeping ceremonies but no human power can force them to keep the moral law. Paul is arguing that we cannot be justified in God's sight by trying to keep the moral law, or the ceremonial law. Eating and drinking and such things in themselves neither justify nor condemn us.

I will go further and state that Paul means the whole law and not any particular part of it as still binding on men. If the law was no longer binding on men because Christ died, all that Paul needed to do was to say so and nothing more. In Galatians 3:10 Paul wrote: 'All who rely on observing the law are under a curse, for it is written: "Cursed is everyone who does not continue to do everything written in the book of the law".' In this text, Paul claims support from Moses that the law is binding on all men and that failure to obey the law puts all men under God's curse.

Neither men who try to keep the law, nor those who do not try to keep it, are justified before God, for they are all spiritually dead. Paul's teaching is that there are two classes of people in the world — those who are spiritual and those who are not (see Romans 3:21 and 28). This is in harmony with the teaching of Jesus Christ in John 3:6: 'Flesh gives birth to flesh but the Spirit gives birth to spirit'. To people who do not have the Holy Spirit, the law is useless. No matter how much they try to keep the law, they will not be justified except by spiritual faith.

Finally, then: if there is such a thing as 'free-will', it must be the noblest thing in a man, for without the Holy Spirit 'free-will' helps a man to keep the whole law! But Paul says that those who are 'of the works of the law' are not justified. This means that this 'free-will' at its best is unable to make men right with God. In fact, in Romans 3:20 Paul says that the law is necessary to show us what sin is. 'Through the law we become conscious of sin'. Those who are 'of the works of the law' can't recognize what sin really is. The law was not given to show men what they can do but to correct their ideas of what right and wrong are in God's sight. 'Free-will' is blind, for it needs to be taught by the law. It is also powerless, for it fails to justify anyone in God's sight.

Argument 4:   The law is designed to lead men to Christ by giving a knowledge of sin

The argument in favour of 'free-will' is that the law would not have been given if we were not able to obey it. Erasmus! You repeatedly say: 'If we can do nothing, what is the purpose of all the laws, precepts, threats and promises?' The answer is that the law was not given to show us what we can do. It was not even given to help us do what is right. Paul says, in Romans 3:20: 'Through the law we become conscious of sin'. The law's purpose is to show what sin is and what it leads to — death, hell and the wrath of God. The law can only point these things out. It cannot free us from them. Deliverance comes only through Jesus Christ, revealed to us in the gospel. Neither reason nor 'free-will' can lead men to Christ, for reason and 'free-will' themselves need the light of the law to show them their own sickness. Paul asks this question in Galatians 3:19: 'What then was the purpose of the law?' But Paul's answer to his own question is the opposite to

21

yours and Jerome's. You say that the law was given to prove the existence of 'free-will'. Jerome says that it was to restrain sin. But Paul does not say either of those things. His whole argument is that men need special grace to fight the evil which the law exposes. There is no cure until the disease is diagnosed. The law is necessary to make men see their dangerous condition so they will long for the remedy that is found only in Christ. So Paul's words in Romans 3:20 may seem to be very simple but they have enough power to make 'free-will' utterly and completely non-existent. Paul says in Romans 7:7: 'I would not have known what it was to covet if the law had not said "Do not covet".' This means that 'free-will' does not even know what sin is! How then can 'free-will' ever know what is right? And if it doesn't know what is right, how can it strive to do what is right?

Argument 5: The doctrine of salvation by faith in Christ proves 'free-will' to be false

In Romans 3:21—25 Paul confidently proclaims: 'But now a righteousness from God, apart from law, has been made known, to which the law and the prophets testify. This righteousness from God comes through faith in Jesus Christ to all who believe. There is no difference, for all have sinned and fall short of the glory of God and are justified freely by his grace through the redemption that came by Christ Jesus. God presented him as a sacrifice of atonement, through faith in his blood'. These words are thunderbolts against 'free-will'. Paul distinguishes the righteousness that God gives from a righteousness that comes from keeping the law. 'Free-will' could only possibly

22

flourish if man could be saved by keeping the law. But Paul clearly demonstrates that we are saved without relying in any way on the works of the law. No matter how much we might imagine a supposed 'free-will' would be able to do good works or make us good citizens, Paul would still say that the righteousness that God gives is a different thing altogether. It is impossible for 'free-will' to survive the assault of verses like these.

These verses also fire another thunderbolt against 'free-will'. In them, Paul draws a line between believers and unbelievers (Romans 3:22). Nobody can deny that the supposed power of 'free-will' is quite different from faith in Jesus Christ. But without faith in Christ, Paul says nothing can be acceptable to God. And if a thing is not acceptable to God, it is sin. It cannot be neutral. Therefore 'free-will', if it exists, is sin because it is opposed to faith and it gives no glory to God.

Romans 3:23 is another thunderbolt. Paul doesn't say: 'all have sinned, except those who do good works by their own "free-will".' There are no exceptions. If it were possible to make ourselves acceptable to God by 'free-will' then Paul is a liar. He ought to have allowed for exceptions. But he states clearly that because of sin, no-one can truly glorify and please God. Anyone who does please God must know that God is pleased with them. But our experience teaches us that nothing in us pleases God. Ask those who argue for 'free-will' to say whether there is something in them that pleases God. They must admit that there is not. And Paul clearly says there is not.

Even those who believe in 'free-will' must agree with me that they cannot glorify God in their own strength. Even with their 'free-will' they doubt whether they please God. So, I prove, on the testimony of their own conscience, that 'free-will' does not please God. Even with all its powers and efforts, 'free-will' is guilty of the sin of unbelief. So we see that the doctrine of salvation by faith is quite contrary to any idea of 'free-will'.

Argument 6: There is no place for any idea of merit or reward

Those who teach 'free-will' say that if there is no 'free-will' then there is no place for merit or reward.

What will the supporters of 'free-will' say about the word 'freely' in Romans 3:24? Paul says that believers are 'freely justified by his grace'. What do they make of 'by his grace'? If salvation is free, and given by grace, it cannot be earned or deserved. Yet Erasmus argues that a man must be able to do something to earn his salvation or he would not deserve to be saved. He thinks that the reason why God justifies one person and not another is because one used his 'free-will' and tried to be righteous and the other didn't. This makes God a respecter of persons and the Bible says he isn't (Acts 10:34). Erasmus and some other persons like him say that men can only do a very little with their own 'free-will' to get salvation. They say that 'free-will' only has a little merit – it doesn't deserve very much. But they still think that 'free-will' makes it possible for people to try to find God. And they still think that if people don't try to find God, it's their own fault if they don't receive his grace.

So whether this 'free-will' has great merit or little, the result is the same. The grace of God is earned by it. But Paul denies all merit when he says we are 'freely' justified. Those who say that 'free-will' has only little merit are just as bad as those who say it has great merit. Both teach that 'free-will' has enough merit to secure the favour of God. So they are really no different from one another.

Actually these supporters of 'free-will' have given us a perfect example of 'jumping out of the frying pan into the fire'. By talking about 'free-will' only having little merit, they make their position worse, not better. At least those who talk about great merit (they are called 'Pelagians') put a high price on God's grace because great merit is needed to earn salvation. But Erasmus makes grace cheap. It can be obtained by a feeble effort. But Paul reduces both ideas to pulp by this one word 'freely' in Romans 3:24. Later, in Romans 11:6 he states that our acceptance with God is only by grace: 'And if by grace, then it is no longer by works; if it were, grace would no longer be grace'. Paul's teaching is quite plain. There is no such thing as human merit in God's sight, whether the merit is great or small. No-one deserves to be saved. No-one can work to be saved. Paul excludes all supposed works of 'free-will' and establishes grace alone. We cannot give ourselves even one tiny bit of credit for our salvation. It is entirely because of God's grace.

Argument 7:   'Free-will' has no value because works have nothing to do with a man's righteousness before God

Now I will follow through with Paul's arguments in Romans 4:2–3: 'If, in fact, Abraham was justified by works, he had something to boast about — but not before God. What does the scripture say? "Abraham believed God and it was credited to him as

25

righteousness".' Now Paul does not deny that Abraham was a righteous man. The whole point is that this righteousness did not earn him salvation. No-one disagrees that evil works are not acceptable to God. That is obvious. The argument is that not even good works make us acceptable to God. They merit his wrath, not his favour. In Romans 4:4—5 Paul sets 'a man who works' over against 'a man who does not work'. Righteousness, which is acceptance with God, is not accounted to 'him who works' but to 'him who does not work' but trusts in God. There is no half-way position.

Argument 8: A whole fistful of arguments

I must mention in passing some more arguments against 'free-will'. I will only refer to them briefly but each of them by itself could completely destroy the idea of 'free-will'.

For example, the source of the grace by which we are saved is God's eternal purpose. This must rule out the suggestion that God is gracious to us because of something we may do.

Another argument is based on the fact that God promised salvation by grace (to Abraham) before he gave the law. Paul argues (Romans 4:13—15; Galatians 3:15—21) that if we are now saved by keeping the law by 'free-will', then this would mean the promise of salvation by grace is cancelled. Faith, also, would have no value.

Paul also tells us that the law can only expose sin, it cannot remove it. Because 'free-will' can only operate on the basis of keeping the law, there can be no righteousness acceptable to God achieved by it.

Lastly, we are all under God's condemnation because

of Adam's sinful disobedience. We all come under this condemnation at our birth, including those who have 'free-will' — if any such people exist! How, then, can 'free-will' help us except to sin and earn condemnation?

I could have left out these arguments and simply given a running commentary on Paul's writings. But I wanted to show just how stupid my opponents are, who fail to see such simple things plainly. I leave them to think over these arguments for themselves.

Argument 9: Paul is absolutely clear in refuting 'free-will'

Paul's arguments are so clear, it is amazing that anyone could misunderstand him. He says: 'They are *all* gone out of the way, there is *none* righteous, none that doeth good, no, not one'. I am amazed that some people say: 'Some are not gone out of the way, are not unrighteous, are not evil, are not sinners; there is something in man that strives after good'. And Paul does not make these statements in a few isolated passages. He makes them sometimes positively and sometimes negatively, by plain statements and by contrasts. The plain meaning of his words, the whole context and the entire scope of his argument, unite in this — that apart from faith in Christ there is nothing but sin and condemnation. My opponents are defeated even if they will not surrender! But that is not in my power to bring about. I must leave that to the work of the Holy Spirit.

Argument 10: The state of man without the Spirit shows that 'free-will' can do nothing spiritual

In Romans 8:5 Paul divides mankind into two — those

of the 'flesh' (or the sinful nature) and those of the 'Spirit' (see also John 3:6). This can only mean that those who do not have the Spirit are in the flesh and still have a sinful nature. Paul says that 'if anyone does not have the Spirit of Christ he does not belong to Christ' (Romans 8:9). This obviously means that those without the Spirit belong to Satan. 'Free-will' hasn't been much good to them! Paul says that 'those controlled by their sinful nature cannot please God' (Romans 8:8). He says that 'the sinful mind is hostile to God. It does not submit to God's law, nor can it do so' (Romans 8:7). It is impossible for such people to make any effort of their own to please God.

A man called Origen suggested that each man has a 'soul' which has the ability to turn to the 'flesh' or to the 'Spirit'. This is just his imagination. He dreamt it! He has no proof for it at all. In fact there is no middle position. Everything without the Spirit is flesh; and the best activities of the flesh are hostile to God. This is the same as the teaching of Christ in Matthew 7:18 that an evil tree cannot produce good fruit. It is also in harmony with the twin statements of Paul — 'the righteous live by faith' (Romans 1:17) and 'whatever is not of faith is sin' (Romans 14:23). Those who are without faith are not justified, and those who are not justified, are sinners in whom any supposed 'free-will' can only produce evil. So 'free-will' is nothing but a slave of sin, death and Satan. Such 'freedom' is no freedom at all.

Argument 11: Those who come to know Christ did not previously think about him, seek him, or prepare themselves for him

In Romans 10:20, Paul quotes Isaiah 65:1: 'I revealed

myself to those who did not ask for me; I was found by those who did not seek me. To a nation that did not call on my name, I said: "Here am I, here am I".' Paul knew from his own experience that he didn't seek God's grace but received it in spite of his furious rage against it. Paul says in Romans 9:30—31 that the Jews who made great efforts to keep the law were not saved by those efforts but Gentiles who are totally ungodly received God's mercy. This clearly shows that all the efforts of a man's 'free-will' are useless to save him. The Jews' zeal got them nowhere, while ungodly Gentiles received salvation. Grace is freely given to the undeserving and unworthy and is not gained by any of the efforts that even the best and most upright of men try to make.

Argument 12: Salvation for a sinful world is by the grace of Christ through faith alone

Let us now turn to John who also writes eloquently against 'free-will'. In John 1:5 he says: 'The light shines in the darkness, but the darkness has not understood (or overcome) it'; and in John 1:10—11: 'He was in the world, and though the world was made through him, the world did not recognise him. He came to that which was his own but his own did not receive him'. By the 'world' John means the whole human race. Since 'free-will' would be a most excellent thing in man, it must be included in whatever John says about the 'world'. Therefore, according to these two texts, 'free-will' does not know the light of truth and it hates Christ and his people. Many other passages, such as John 7:7; 8:23; 14:7; 15:19;

I John 2:16; 5:19, proclaim that the 'world' (and that especially includes 'free-will') is under Satan's command.

The 'world' includes all that is not separated to God by the Spirit. Now, if there had been anybody in the world who had by 'free-will' known the truth and by 'free-will' did not hate Christ, John would have altered what he wrote. But he didn't do so. It is clear, therefore, that 'free-will' is as guilty as the 'world'. In John 1:12—13 John goes on: 'Yet to all who received him, to those who believed in his name, he gave the right to become children of God — children born not of natural descent, nor of human decision, or a husband's will, but born of God'. 'Not of natural descent' means it is useless to rely on your place of birth, or on your family. 'Nor of human decision' means it is foolish to rely on the 'works of the law'. 'Or of a husband's will' means that no effort by man can begin to make him acceptable to God.

If 'free-will' is useful at all, John ought not to reject 'human decision' or else he's in danger of Isaiah 5:20: 'Woe to those who call good evil'. There can be no doubt that natural birth is of no use to gain salvation because in Romans 9:8 Paul writes: 'It is not the natural children who are God's children, but it is the children of promise'.

Then John also says in John 1:16: 'From the fulness of his grace we have all received one blessing after another'. So we receive spiritual blessings only through the grace of another and not by our own efforts. Two opposite things cannot both be true — that grace is so cheap, anyone, anywhere can earn it, and at the same time grace is so dear that we can only receive it through the merit of one man, Jesus Christ.

I wish my opponents would realise that when they

argue for 'free-will' they are denying Christ. If we can obtain grace by 'free-will', we do not need Christ. And if we have Christ, we do not need 'free-will'. Supporters of 'free-will' prove their denial of Christ by their action, because some of them even resort to the intercession of Mary and the 'saints' and fail to rely on Christ as the only mediator between man and God. They all abandon Christ in his work as mediator and the kindest Saviour and regard the merits of Christ as of less value than their own efforts.

Argument 13: The case of Nicodemus in John 3 opposes 'free-will'

Look at Nicodemus' virtues (John 3:1–2). He confesses Christ to be true and to have come from God. He refers to Christ's miracles. He seeks out Christ to hear more from him. Now when he hears of the new birth (John 3:3–8), does he admit that this is what he had sought in the past? No! He is startled and confused and he turns away from it at first as an impossibility (John 3:9). Even the greatest philosophers have to admit that they do not know about Christ; much less can they seek those things that belong to salvation, before Christ came. When they admit that, they are admitting that their 'free-will' is ignorant and powerless! Surely, those who teach 'free-will' are crazy, but they will not keep quiet and give glory to God.

Argument 14: 'Free-will' is useless because salvation is by Christ alone

It is clear from John 14:6 where Christ is said to be

'the Way, the Truth and the Life' that salvation is to be found only in Jesus Christ. That being so, everything out of Christ can only be dark, false and dead. What need would there be for Christ to come if men naturally understood the way to God, knew God's truth, and shared God's life?

Our opponents say that bad men have 'free-will' even though they abuse it. If this is so, then there is something good in the worst of men. And if that is so, then God is unjust to condemn them. But John says that those who do not believe in Jesus Christ are condemned already (John 3:18). But if men possess this good thing called 'free-will', then John ought to have said that they are condemned only because of their bad part, not because of this good part in them. Scripture says: 'Whoever rejects the Son will not see life, for God's wrath remains on him' (John 3:36). This must mean the whole of a man. If this were not so, then there would be a part in a man preventing him from being condemned and he could go on sinning without any fears, secure in the knowledge that he cannot be condemned.

Again, we read in John 3:27 that 'a man can receive only what is given him from heaven'. This refers especially to a man's ability to do God's will. Only what comes from above can help a man to do God's will. But 'free-will' does not come from above, which means that 'free-will' is useless.

In John 3:31 John says: 'The one who is from the earth belongs to the earth and speaks as one from the earth; the one who comes from heaven is above all'. Now, 'free-will' certainly has no heavenly origin. It is of the earth and there is no other possibility. This can only mean, therefore, that 'free-will' has nothing to do with heavenly things. It can only be concerned with earthly things. Christ says, in John 8:23: 'You are from below, I am from above. You are of this world, I am not of this world'. If this statement only meant that their bodies were of the world, the statement would not be necessary, for they knew that already. Christ means that they were totally lacking in any spiritual power and this could only come from God.

Argument 15: Man is unable to believe the gospel, so all his efforts cannot save him

In John 6:44 Christ says: 'No-one can come to me unless the Father who sent me draws him'. This leaves absolutely no room for 'free-will'. The Lord goes on to explain the Father's drawing: 'Everyone who listens to the Father and learns from him, comes to me' (verse 45). Man's will, left to itself, is powerless to do anything about coming to Christ for salvation. Even the very word of the gospel is heard in vain, unless the Father himself speaks to the heart and draws us to Christ. Erasmus wants to play down the plain meaning of this text by likening men to sheep who respond to the shepherd when he holds out a branch to them. He argues that there is something in men that responds to the gospel. But this will not do, because even if God shows the gift of his own Son to ungodly men, they don't respond unless he works within them. Indeed, without the Father's inward working, men are more likely to persecute his Son rather than follow him. But, when the Father shows how wonderful his Son is to those to whom he has given understanding, then they are drawn to him. Such people are already 'sheep' and they know the shepherd's voice!

Argument 16: Universal unbelief proves 'free-will' to be false

In John 16:8 Jesus says that the Holy Spirit will 'convict the world of guilt in regard to sin'. In verse 9 he explains that the sin is 'men do not believe in me'. Now this sin of unbelief is not in the skin or in the hair, but in the mind and the will. All men without exception are as ignorant of the fact of their guilty unbelief as they are ignorant of Christ himself. The guilt of unbelief has to be revealed to them by the Holy Spirit. So all that is in man, including 'free-will', stands condemned by God and can only add to the guilt of which he is ignorant until God shows it to him. The whole of scripture proclaims Christ as the only way of salvation. Anyone who is outside Christ is under the power of Satan, sin, death and the wrath of God. Christ alone can rescue men from the kingdom of Satan. We are not delivered by any power within us but only by the grace of God.

Argument 17: The power of the 'flesh' in true believers disproves 'free-will'

For some reason you ignore my arguments from Romans 7 and Galatians 5. These two chapters show us that even in true christian believers the power of the 'flesh' is such that they cannot do what they know they should do and want to do. Human nature is so bad even in people who have the Spirit of God in them, that not only do they fail to do what is right but they even fight against it. What possibility can there be then that there is a power in those who are not born again to do good? As Paul says in Romans 8:7: 'The carnal mind is enmity against God'. I would like to meet the man who can puncture that argument!

Argument 18: Knowing that salvation does not depend on 'free-will' can be very comforting

I confess that I wouldn't want 'free-will' even if it were given to me! If my salvation were left to me I would be no match for all the dangers, difficulties and devils that I have to fight. But even if there were no enemies to fight, I could never be certain of success. I would never be sure I had pleased God or whether there was something more I needed to do. I can prove this from my own painful experience over many years. But my salvation is in God's hands and not my own. He will be faithful to his promise to save me, not on the basis of what I do but according to his great mercy. God does not lie and will not let my enemy the devil snatch me out of his hands. By 'free-will', not one person can be saved. But by free grace, many will be saved. Not only so, but I am glad to know that as a christian I please God, not because of what I do but because of his grace. If I work too little or too badly he graciously pardons me and makes me better. This is the glory of all Christians.

Argument 19: God's honour cannot be tarnished

You may be worried that it is hard to defend the honour of God in all this. 'After all', you might say, 'he condemns those who cannot help being sinful and who are forced to stay that way because God does not choose to save them'. As Paul says: 'Like the rest, we were by nature objects of wrath' (Ephesians 2:3). But you must look at it another way. God should be reverenced and respected as one who is merciful to all he justifies and saves, although they are completely unworthy. We know God is divine. He is also wise and just. His justice is not the same as human justice. It is beyond our human understanding to grasp fully, as Paul exclaims in Romans 11:33: 'Oh the depth of the riches of the wisdom and knowledge of God! How unsearchable his judgments and his paths beyond tracing out!' If we agree that God's nature, strength, wisdom and knowledge are far above ours, we should also believe that his justice is greater and better than ours. He has promised us that when he reveals his glory to us, we will see clearly what we should believe now – that he is just, always was and always will be.

Here is another example. If you use human reason to consider the way God rules the affairs of the world, you are forced to say either that there is no God or that God is unjust. The wicked prosper and the good suffer (see Job 12:6 and Psalm 73:12) and that appears to be unjust. So, many men deny the existence of God and say that everything happens by chance. The answer to this problem is that there is life after this life and all that is not punished and repaid here will be punished and repaid there. This life is nothing more than a preparation for, or rather, a beginning of the life that is to come. This problem has been debated in every age but is never solved, except by believing the gospel as found in the Bible. Three lights shine on the problem: the light of nature, the light of grace and the light of glory. By the light of nature, God seems to be unjust for the good suffer and the wicked prosper. The light of grace helps us further but it does not explain how God can condemn someone who, by his own strength,

36

can do nothing but sin and be guilty. Only the light of glory will explain this on that coming day when God will reveal himself as a God who is entirely just, although his judgment is beyond the understanding of human beings. A godly man believes that God fore-knows and fore-ordains all things and that nothing happens except by his will. No man, or angel, or any other creature, therefore, has a 'free-will'. Satan is the prince of this world and holds all men captive unless they are released by the power of the Holy Spirit.

Chapter Two

What Erasmus taught.

Argument 1: Erasmus' definition of 'free-will'

To be fair I must quote your own definition of 'free-will'. You say: 'I understand free-will to be a power of the human will by which a man may apply himself to those things that lead to eternal salvation or to turn away from them'.

You cannot really call this a definition! A definition should be clear, but each part of this statement has to be explained to make it clear. Also, you set out to define one thing but end up by defining something quite different. I mean that only God has the freedom of will that you describe and yet you reckon it belongs to men. But a man is like a slave whose only freedom is to obey his master. Men only act according to God's commands. Is that 'freedom of the will' as you describe it?

Now I must take this so-called definition apart. Some parts are clear enough, but I have to force other parts into the open before I can attack them. They seem to be afraid of the light as though they are guilty of something! I will begin by supposing that the 'power of the human will' you speak of, is a power to choose or to reject something, a power to approve or disapprove. This is indeed the function of man's will.

But you add: 'by which a man may apply himself . . .' What you are doing is to separate a man from his will. You give a man power to direct his will. But a man's will is part of himself — it is the part of him that makes these choices. Clearly, to separate a man from his will and give him power over his will, is absurd! If I have misunderstood you, that is your fault for not writing more plainly!

Now what are the things that 'lead to eternal salvation'? They must be the words and works of God. Nothing else can lead us to eternal salvation. But the human mind cannot grasp the meaning of salvation. Paul says: 'No eye has seen, no ear has heard, no mind conceived what God has prepared for those who love him'. Then he goes on to say how we can know such things — 'God has revealed it to us by his Spirit'. This must mean that without the Spirit we could never know this salvation and so we could not 'apply' ourselves to it.

Some of the most educated men this world has known have regarded spiritual things as nonsense. In fact, the more brilliant their minds, the more ridiculous spiritual truth appeared to them. Men can only know the reality of spiritual things in their hearts because the Holy Spirit enlightens them.

Next, you inform us that 'free-will' is a power of the human will which can, by itself, decide to receive or not to receive the word and the work of God. This is to make the human will able to choose heaven or hell. It means there is no room for the Holy Spirit or for God's grace. This is to put the human will on a level with God.

Those people called Pelagians did this, too. But you improve on them! They divided 'free-will' into two parts — the power to *understand* the difference between things and the power to *choose* between them. But your 'free-will' has the one power to choose eternal things which it is completely unable to understand. You have created a 'half free-will'!

And you are contradicting yourself, too, because you once said that 'the human will can do nothing without grace'. But when you come to writing a definition of 'free-will', you allow complete freedom to man's will. You are really a very strange man!

I prefer the teachings of some of the old philosophers to yours. They said that a man left to himself will only do wrong. Man could only choose good with the help of grace. They said men were free to go down but needed help to go up! But it is laughable to call that 'free-will'. On those grounds I could say a stone has 'free-will' because it can only go down unless it is lifted up by someone! The teaching of the philosophers is better than yours. Your stone can choose to go both down and up!

Argument 2: Erasmus' argument from a book in the Apocrypha

You argue your case for 'free-will' from Ecclesiasticus 15:14—17. 'God from the beginning made man and left him in the hand of his own counsel'. The writer also adds the following words about God's commandments and precepts: 'If you are willing to keep my commandments and to keep continually the faith that pleases me, they will preserve you. He has set before you fire and water; upon which you will stretch forth your hand. Before man is life and death; and whichever pleases him shall be given to him'.

I could dismiss this supposed proof-text by saying

that Ecclesiasticus was not included by the Jews in the Old Testament, but it is enough that you yourself describe it as 'obscure and ambiguous'. It would take an eternity for you, or anyone else for that matter, to produce a passage that tells us plainly what 'free-will' is.

Argument 3: Erasmus' three views about 'free-will'

You produce three views about 'free-will' out of one! Let us look at them. The first is the view that man cannot will to do good; he cannot start it, make progress in it or finish it, without special grace. You call this view 'severe, but probable enough'.

The second, which you regard as 'more severe', is that 'free-will' can only lead to sin and that grace alone can lead to goodness.

The third, which you say is 'most severe', is that 'free-will' is meaningless and that God is the cause of both good and evil in us.

You are prepared to accept the first of these views because it allows to man some effort that he can make. You say you are opposed to the other two views. You do not seem to know what you are talking about! These are not three different views. They are the same view put in different words at different times by your opponents. Your definition of 'free-will' is nothing like the first view that you say is acceptable. Your definition says that 'free-will' can do both bad and good. But the view you accept says that man's will can't choose the good without the help of God's grace. You now have two wills at loggerheads. By accepting the first view, you agree that 'free-will' cannot do good. A little earlier you had said: 'The

44

human will is so bad that it has lost its freedom and is forced to serve sin and cannot get back to a better state'. Yet when I say exactly the same thing, you say: 'Nothing so absurd was ever heard of'. What you write means that trying to be good is both in the power of 'free-will' and not in the power of 'free-will' at one and the same time. If this isn't a freak, I would like to know what is!

Your statements are so opposite to each other that there is no possibility of them holding together. There is no middle ground between 'able to do good' and 'not able to do good'.

As for the second and third views that you outlined, there is nothing in them that is not found in the first. All three are in perfect harmony. You say you oppose only the second and third views but all three plainly say that the human will has lost its freedom; it is bound to the service of sin and can will no good. Now if this is true, it follows that when man does evil, he does so because he must. He cannot help it.

Argument 4: Return to Erasmus' argument from Ecclesiasticus 15:14–17

Let us return to this passage from the Apocrypha and compare it with the first of the three views we have just referred to. This view, which you think is probably right, states that 'free-will' cannot will to do good. But the passage from Ecclesiasticus is quoted to prove that 'free-will' can do some good. According to you, this passage ought to support the first view but it says nothing about that at all. You might as well quote a passage about Pilate as Governor of Syria to prove that Christ was Messiah!

45

But to be fair, we will look at Ecclesiasticus 15:14—17. The passage begins: 'God from the beginning made man and left him in the hand of his own counsel'. Up to this point there is no reference to commandments. Man's will was entirely free when God made him lord of all things. But then God is said to have added his commandments and precepts, saying: 'If you are willing to keep my commandments . . .' This also is true. God took man from his place of dominion and from then on he was under God's commands. He was not free. So you see it is possible to understand this passage in a way that agrees with me and not with you! My understanding of the passage agrees with the whole of scripture. Your understanding of it puts this one text against the whole of scripture.

Argument 5: Further examination of Erasmus' use of Ecclesiasticus 15:14—17

You suggest that the words 'If you are willing to keep' show that man is able to choose freely. To argue like that is to judge God's words by human reason. But I can prove that even according to human reason, the words 'if you are willing' do not always mean an ability to obey. For example, parents often tell their children to do something, not to prove what they *can* do, but to prove what they *cannot* do, so that they will learn to call for help.

This is how God deals with us. He gives us his law, to expose our complete inability to keep it. This is the teaching of Paul in Romans 3:20; 5:20; Galatians 3:19, 24.

Argument 6: Erasmus' arguments must mean that man's will is completely free

There is a basic contradiction in your argument. On the one hand, you say the words from Ecclesiasticus 15:14—17 ('if you are willing to keep . . .') mean that a man can freely will, or not will. But you also say that the first of the three possible views you have stated is probably true. But that view said that 'free-will' cannot do any good. You cannot have it both ways!

Now Ecclesiasticus does not say: 'if you will desire and try to keep my commandments . . .' It says: 'if you are willing to keep my commandments . . .' If Ecclesiasticus, therefore, is in favour of 'free-will' at all, it must be a complete freedom and not something only half-way. This is the conclusion those people called Pelagians reach about these words.

Anyone who wants to disagree with the Pelagians will have a big problem. That person may only want a little 'free-will' in the passage, as you do. That means that a man is merely free to desire and try to obey God. The Pelagians would answer by saying either that the passage teaches total 'free-will' or total bondage of the will. And they would take the argument even further, for the passage says: 'if you will keep the faith . . .' As a result, they teach that man is also free to believe. But Paul in the scriptures argues strongly against that, for he says that faith is the special gift of God (Ephesians 2:8).

But I must return to my argument that Ecclesiasticus does not teach 'free-will'. It is quite wrong to argue that the words 'if you are willing' must mean 'therefore you can'. The first man, Adam, was assisted by God's grace and yet he disobeyed. If Adam disobeyed, what can we do before we have any grace at all? 'Free-will' is totally powerless. If you put Adam's situation alongside Ecclesiasticus 15:14-17 you will see that this passage, far from being in favour of 'free-will' is a most powerful argument against it. This passage teaches our duty to do God's will and not our ability to obey God.

Argument 7: Genesis 4:7 — another text to prove that a command does not mean ability to obey

This text is: 'sin is crouching at your door; it desires to have you, but you must master it'. You quote these words to prove that evil thoughts can be overcome and need not lead to actual sin. Once again you contradict yourself. You have already said that the view that is probably true is the view which says that man's will cannot will what is good. Yet here you say that man can overcome evil desires without a single reference to the help of Christ or the Holy Spirit.

The text is, in fact, teaching nothing of the sort. It is another example of man being shown what he *ought* to do and not what he *can* do. Another example is the first commandment — 'You shall have no other gods before me'. Texts are commands, and commands do not imply an ability to obey. Rather, they expose inability, as in the case of Cain.

Argument 8: Deuteronomy 30:19 — 'the law is designed to give knowledge of sin'

This is the third passage you quote in favour of 'free-will'. It reads: 'I have set before you life and death, blessings and curses. Now choose life'. You say: 'What could be clearer than that a man has freedom of choice?' But I reply that you are blind! When Moses said: 'choose life', did the people choose it? If they had done so, there would have been no need of the work of the Holy Spirit.

You say: 'It is ridiculous to say to a man standing where two roads meet, "Go which way you like" when only one is open to him'. What a foolish illustration! It is true that we stand at a road junction but both roads — not only one — are closed to us. We are unable to get on the road that leads to good, without God's grace. We can't even take the other road without God's permission! In Romans 3:20 Paul does not say: 'Through the law we become conscious of power or goodness'. He does not say: 'Through the law is the power of will'. He says: 'Through the law we become conscious of sin'. The law does not say what men *can* do, but what they *should* do.

You then quote from Deuteronomy 3 about 'choosing', 'turning away' and 'keeping'. You say that if people don't actually have the power to do these things, then the commands are pointless. But again, all these commands say what people ought to do. They are not pointless. They are designed to teach proud man how powerless he is. You try to ridicule this position by likening it to a man who is tied-up except for his left arm. He is told there is good wine to his right and poison to his left. He is then told to choose one of them. What are you trying to prove by this picture? Are you trying to prove the absolute freedom of man's will? You are so forgetful! You have already said that 'free-will' can do nothing without God's grace. You have tried to ridicule my position by your illustration, but let me put my position by a better illustration. Here is a man who has both arms bound! This man boasts that he is free to move his arms to the right and to the left. So he is commanded to move in one direction — not to make fun of him, but to prove that he can't do it. In the scripture we see man not only bound by Satan but also fooled into thinking that he is free to do what is right. The law of Moses was given to show men that they are fooled by their imagined freedom.

Argument 9: Erasmus' confusion of law and gospel

You take up a number of passages to prove your case but you fail completely to show the difference between the law and the gospel. Let me show you how the gospel is taught in passages you think refer to the law. For instance, look at Jeremiah 15:19: 'If you will turn, then will I turn you', and Zechariah 1:3: 'Turn to me, says the Lord of hosts, and I will turn to you'. Does 'turn' prove that a man has the ability to turn, any more than 'Love the Lord your God with all the heart' (Deuteronomy 6:5) proves that he has the ability to love God? These words do *not* prove that men can turn to God by their own power. But when men know what they *should* do, then they will ask where they can find the ability to obey. The words 'Turn to me' do not mean 'Try to turn'. You say that grace is available when men try to turn. But that would make the second part of those verses also mean 'I will try to turn to you'! That would be astonishing! Perhaps grace would be available to God, too!

Away with these empty arguments! The word 'turn' is used in scripture both in a 'legal' way and in an 'evangelical' way. When it is used in a legal way, it is a command demanding, not only that a man try to obey, but, a complete change of his life (e.g. Jeremiah 4:1; 25:5; 35:15). When the word 'turn' is used in its evangelical sense it is spoken by God as a comfort and promise, in which nothing is required of us but the grace of God is offered to us (e.g. Psalm 14:7; 116:7; 126:1). Zechariah has set before us the message of both law and grace. The whole of the law is summed up in the words 'Turn to me' and grace is summed up in the words 'I will turn to you'.

You treat Ezekiel 18:23 in the same way. 'As surely as I live, declares the Sovereign Lord, I take no pleasure in the death of the wicked, but rather that they turn from their ways and live'. Once again you take the words 'that they turn' to imply ability to do so. You make this text law instead of gospel. You make it a demand that we should not sin. That is law. But the Lord says: 'I take no pleasure in the death of the wicked' and speaks plainly of the punishment of sin which the sinner deserves and realizes. God is giving such a person hope of pardon and salvation. The words of the law are laid heavily on those who neither feel nor know their sins. They are shown what they ought to do. But then the gospel is addressed to those who are distressed by a sense of sin and are tempted to despair.

So these words from Ezekiel: 'I take no pleasure in the death of the wicked', far from proving 'free-will', prove the very opposite. They show how helpless we are apart from God's words of promise. Indeed, we grow worse, until grace raises us up. These words of mercy are necessary to save sinners (unless, that is, you think that God says these things because he likes talking). No-one will receive this word of promise but he to whom the law has shown his sin. Those who have not felt the power of God's law and have no fear of death and judgement, have no interest in God's promises of mercy.

Argument 10: God's revealed will and his secret will

In the passage from Ezekiel that we have just considered, the prophet does not deal at all with the question as to why some people are convicted by the law and others are not. Nor does he deal with why some receive God's grace and others do not.

We must make a clear distinction between God's revealed will and God's secret will. God, in his secret will, plans that those whom he chooses will receive his mercy. We are not to enquire into this but to adore with reverence. We are to be concerned with what God has revealed to us and not with what he keeps to himself.

Applied to our text, this means that God, hidden in majesty, does not regret the death of the sinner. But God, as he is revealed to men, grieves over the death he finds in his people and has acted so that sin and death may be taken away. It is impossible for us to be guided by the secret will of God, for we cannot know what it is. It is enough for us to know that God's secret will exists so that we may fear and adore him.

So it is quite right to say that it is our fault if we perish, if we are speaking of God as he is made known to us, for the fault is indeed in the will of man (Matthew 23:27). But why God does not remove this fault in every man, or why God makes us responsible for the fault when we cannot avoid it, is not for us to ask. Even if we ask, we will not find the answer, as Paul says in Romans 9:20: 'Who are you, O man, to talk back to God?'

Argument 11: Obligation is no evidence of ability to obey

You go on to argue: 'If it is not in the power of every man to keep what is commanded, all the encouragements in the scriptures, all the promises, threats, rebukes, blessings, curses and dozens of examples, are of necessity useless'. But, as I have explained many times, passages of scripture which demand a duty cannot be used to prove the existence of such a 'free-will' as you suggest.

One of the last passages you use to support your position is Deuteronomy 30:11—14: 'Now what I am commanding you today is not too difficult for you or beyond your reach. It is not up in heaven, so that you have to ask "Who will ascend into heaven to get it and proclaim it to us so that we may obey it?" Nor is it beyond the sea, so that you have to ask "Who will cross the sea to get it and proclaim it to us so that we may obey it?" No, the word is very near you; it is in your mouth and in your heart so that you may obey it'.

You say that these words show, not only that it is possible for us to do what we are commanded to do, but that it is as easy as falling off a log! But if that is really the meaning of this passage, then we have to say that Christ was a fool to waste his time. He shed his blood to obtain the Holy Spirit for us when all the time we don't need him, for we can easily and naturally do all that God requires. But if this is the case, how does it square with your own argument that the view that 'free-will' can do no good without grace is probably true? Have you forgotten that you wrote that?

So I hardly need to refer to Paul's explanation of Deuteronomy 30:11—14 in Romans 10:8. I need only look at the passage itself to see that not a word is said about 'free-will' in it. For instance, what do the words 'difficult for you', 'beyond your reach', 'in heaven' and 'beyond the sea' mean? They merely refer to things we might try to do. They say nothing about our ability to do these things. They quite simply refer to distance. I know all this is schoolboy logic, but what else can I do when I am faced with such foolish arguments? Quite plainly, Moses in this passage is a faithful law-giver. He leaves the people with no excuse for not knowing what the law of God is. They need look no-where else to know what God requires. They cannot plead ignorance as an excuse for not keeping the law. They cannot say it is all a mystery. It is there plainly to be seen. So 'free-will' has all its excuses for dis-obedience taken away from it.

I repeat that these texts show us only what God requires. They show us what we ought to do but cannot do. They are intended to show us how power-less and sinful we are.

Argument 12: Man must not pry into the secret will of God

We now come to your New Testament 'proof' texts. You give prominence to Matthew 23:37: 'O Jerusalem, Jerusalem . . . how often I have longed to gather your children together but you were not willing'. You argue that if everything happens exactly as God wills, then Jerusalem might justly reply: 'Why waste your tears? If you didn't intend us to listen to the prophets, why did you send them? Why do you hold us responsible when *you* decided what we should do?'

But, as I have already said, we are not to pry into

54

God's secret will, for the secret things of God are quite beyond us (I Timothy 6:16). We should spend our time considering God incarnate, the Lord Jesus Christ, in whom God has made clear to us what we should and should not know (Colossians 2:3). It is true that the incarnate God says: 'I have longed to gather . . . but you were not willing'. Christ came to do, suffer and offer to all men all that is necessary for salvation. Some men, being hardened by God's secret will, rejected him (John 1:5,11). The same God incarnate weeps and laments over the destruction of the ungodly, even though in his divine will he purposely leaves them to perish. It is not for us to ask why, but to stand in awe of God.

Now some will say that as soon as I am driven into a corner, I dodge the issue by saying we cannot pry into God's secret will. But this is not my invention. It is the way Paul argued in Romans 9:19 and 21; and Isaiah before him (Isaiah 58:2). Clearly we must not try to search out God's secret will, especially when we notice that it is ungodly men who are strongly tempted to do so. We must urge them to be quiet and reverent. If anyone wants to carry on this line of enquiry, he is welcome to, but he will find himself fighting against God. We will watch to see who wins!

Argument 13: The law shows the weakness of man and the saving power of God

Another passage you quote is Matthew 19:17: 'If you want to enter life, obey the commandments'. You ask how the words 'if you want to' could be said to someone whose will is not free. But in one place you have already agreed that 'free-will' can will no good and that without grace it can only serve sin. How can you now want to prove that the will is completely free? Is it really true that every time we say 'if you will' or 'if you want to', it means that there is ability to do the thing? Suppose we say: 'If you want to be compared with David, you must produce psalms like his'. Don't we mean that it is impossible for us, unless God enables us? So, in the scriptures we find expressions like this to show us what can be done in the power of God and what we cannot do by ourselves. These expressions not only show up things we cannot do in our natural strength, they also give promise of a time when these things will be done by the power of God. We can put the meaning of scripture like this: 'If you will ever have the will to keep the commandments (which you will have, not of yourself, but of God who gives it to whom he will), then they will preserve you'.

In this way we can see that we can do none of the things that are commanded and yet at the same time we can do them all — our weaknesses are our own; our abilities come by the grace of God.

Argument 14: Instructions in the New Testament are given to guide those who are justified

You use an argument based on the many references in the New Testament to good works and bad works. For example: 'Rejoice and be glad, because great is your reward in heaven, for in the same way they persecuted the prophets who were before you' (Matthew 5:12). You say that if everything is done because God wills it, there cannot possibly be any merit in good works. So you want the text to mean that man can unaided do good works that will merit reward in heaven. Well,

well! 'Free-will' has made some strides as your book has grown! Not only is 'free-will' able to will and to do good but now you want it to merit eternal life! So what need have we of Christ or the Holy Spirit?

'Clever' men can be blind to things that are quite clear to 'simple' people! You fail to see the difference between the Old Testament and the New Testament. In the Old Testament there are laws and threats that are designed to make us run to the promises found in the New Testament. In the New Testament there is the gospel in which we find grace and the forgiveness of sins obtained for us by Christ crucified. Then there are encouragements and instructions which are intended to stir up those who are justified, having received grace and pardon, to produce the fruit of the Spirit and to carry the cross boldly.

You are blind to the whole regenerating work of the Spirit, seeing in scripture only laws by which men are to live. This is surprising in one who has spent so much time studying scripture. This text (Matthew 5:12) has as much to do with 'free-will' as light has to do with darkness, being designed only to encourage the apostles who were already 'in grace' so that they could endure the troubles of the world.

Argument 15: The basis for reward is the promise of God, not the merit of man

The 'reward' in Matthew 5:12 is a kind of promise. But a promise does not prove that we can do anything. It only proves that if we do certain things we will be rewarded. The question is whether we can do the things for which the reward is given. Some say: the prize is set before all who run, therefore all can run and obtain the prize! Isn't that ridiculous logic? (It

57

would be helpful if 'free-will' could be established by such arguments!)

You try to argue that if God decides everything then we cannot speak of reward. If you mean that you would not 'reward' an unwilling workman, I agree. But when people do good or evil willingly, then reward or punishment properly follow. This is true even though they cannot alter their will by their own strength. If, however, we can will to do what is good only by grace, then clearly the merit and reward are of grace alone.

But we should not talk about merit. Rather, we should talk about the consequences of what we do. There is nothing good or evil that does not have its reward. Hell and the judgment of God certainly and surely await the wicked. In the same way, a kingdom certainly awaits the godly because it has been prepared for them by their Father (Matthew 25:34). If we try to do good in order to merit God's kingdom, we shall fail, proving that we are ungodly. The sons of God do good seeking no reward except the glory of God.

What, then, is the meaning of all the scriptures which promise the kingdom and threaten hell? (Genesis 15:1; II Chronicles 15:7; Job 34:11; Romans 2:7). They simply show the result of a good or a bad life. They are designed to instruct and to awaken. They say nothing about merit but teach us what we should do and encourage us to carry on to the end. (Genesis 15:1; I Corinthians 15:58; 16:13). It is just as though we were to comfort someone by saying that what he does pleases God, or to warn someone that what he does displeases God.

But you argue: 'Why does God bother to tell us these things when they are all settled beforehand?' The answer is that God produces his purpose in us through his Word. He could do these things without that Word but it has pleased him to have us as workers together with him. So he tells us these things in the Word to involve us. So we see that God performs his will in us but he also gives his Word to tell the whole world the facts about rewards and punishments, so that his power and glory and our weakness and wickedness may be proclaimed worldwide. But these truths, which all others despise, are received by the godly in their hearts.

Argument 16: God's sovereignty does not destroy our responsibility

You argue from the words 'by their fruit you will recognise them' (Matthew 7:16) that the fruit is said to be ours and so it cannot be given us by God through his Spirit. This is a silly argument! Christ is said to be ours, even though we received him. Our eyes are ours, even though we did not make them! Then you use another argument from Luke 23:34: 'Father forgive them, for they do not know what they are doing'. You say that if our will is not free then it would have been better for Jesus to excuse his murderers because they had no 'free-will' and could not do otherwise. But the answer is in our Lord's own words: 'They do not know what they are doing'. Could it be plainer that Christ was saying that they were unable to will what is good? How could they will what they didn't know? No stronger statement could be made of the poverty of the will. It not only can do no good but it does not even know how much evil it is doing, nor does it know what good is!

Then, again, you use John 1:12: 'Yet to all who received him, to those who believed in his name, he gave the right to become children of God'. You argue: 'How is the right given to them to become children of God if there is no freedom of the will?' But look carefully at the verse. John speaks of the complete change-over from being a son of the devil to being a son of God. The man does nothing but becomes something! We become children of God by the work of God, not by any exercise of 'free-will' within us. John is telling us that the gospel of grace, without works being required, creates for all men the splendid opportunity of being children of God, if they will believe. But this willing and believing are matters of which they had no previous knowledge. Much less could they do these things by their own strength. Men could not work out for themselves a gospel involving faith on Christ as both Son of God and Son of Man. How then could they be willing or able to receive it? John is not preaching the virtues of 'free-will' but the riches of God's kingdom made known to all the world in the gospel. John also shows how few are those who receive the gospel, for the very reason that 'free-will' opposes it. The power of 'free-will' amounts to this — Satan rules over it so that it rejects God's grace. It also rejects the Spirit who fulfils the law in us, because 'free-will' thinks it can obey the law by its own efforts.

Then you go on to quote Paul to support your case. (Paul, the great opponent of 'free-will'!) You use Romans 2:4: 'Or do you show contempt for the riches of his kindness, tolerance and patience, not realizing that God's kindness should lead you to repentance?' You ask: 'How can those be guilty of despising the things of God who have no 'free-will'? As God is the judge who compels evil-doing, how can he condemn?' Can't you see that these words in Romans 2:4 are a warning, designed to make ungodly men see how powerless they are? Having humbled them, God would prepare such people to receive his grace.

Chapter Three

What Luther thought of Erasmus' teaching.

Argument 1: Erasmus' method

You try to strike fear into your opponents by collecting a large number of texts to support 'free-will'. You then try to make us look foolish by suggesting that we have only two texts on our side — Exodus 9:12 and Malachi 1:2–3. You don't seem to be at all impressed by Paul's handling of these texts in Romans 9!

However, I will take these two texts and show the strong support for our side.

Argument 2: Erasmus' twisting of texts

You have invented a new way of missing the obvious meaning of a text. You insist that texts which clearly oppose 'free-will' must have an 'explanation' to bring out their true meaning. We must insist that such an 'explanation' is only ever necessary when it would be absurd to keep to the plain sense of a text. Everywhere else we should stick to the simple and natural meaning of the words, guided by the rules of grammar and habits of speech God has created among men. If we do otherwise, there will be nothing we can be sure about anywhere. It is not enough to claim that an 'explanation' *may* be needed. In each case we must ask if there *need* be, or *must* be, an 'explanation'. If we cannot prove it to be necessary, we achieve nothing.

An example of your 'explanations' is your treatment of Exodus 4:21: 'I will harden the heart of Pharaoh'. You say that this should mean: 'I will allow it to be hardened', because sometimes we say something like: 'I ruined you', when we mean: 'I did not correct you when you went wrong'. But the meaning of the words is obvious and clear. They need no 'explanation'. The Word of God must be taken in its plain meaning, as the words stand. We are not to re-write the words of God as we please. We might find ourselves 'explaining' the words 'God created the heavens and the earth' to mean 'He set them in place but did not make them out of nothing!' To follow that practice would mean that anyone in the world could be a theologian as soon as he opens his Bible!

Argument 3:   Erasmus' 'explanation' of the hardening of Pharaoh's heart

You interpret 'I will harden the heart of Pharaoh' as meaning: 'My longsuffering, by which I bear with the sinner and which leads others to repentance, just makes Pharaoh more obstinate in wickedness'. You treat Romans 9:18 and Isaiah 63:17 in the same way. But I have only your word that these are the right explanations. True, you quote Origen and Jerome, but who convinces me that they are right?

In short, the result of your 'explanation' is to turn the meaning of these texts upside down. God says: 'I will harden Pharaoh's heart'. You make God say: 'Pharaoh will harden his own heart'. You charge

Pharaoh's hardening of his own heart to the account of God's mercy. If you go on like this, you will turn God's mercy into wrath and God's wrath into mercy. Of course, we know that God's mercy can lead to some people being hardened, but so can his wrath. We know that God's mercy will soften some hearts but so also will his wrath. But this is no excuse for confusing God's wrath and God's mercy. God said he would harden Pharaoh's heart and God afflicted and punished him with ten plagues. But you would make these plagues acts of God's mercy! What more outrageous an idea could be heard! God's mercy was also active when he suspended the plagues over and over again when Pharaoh appeared to repent, but those plagues were the means he used to punish Pharaoh and to harden Pharaoh's heart.

Let us suppose that God does harden hearts when he exercises his longsuffering by withholding immediate punishment. Hearts will still not be softened except by the Spirit of God. Therefore, no matter what process is used, hearts are hardened at the will of God and softened by order of the same divine will.

You say: 'As by the same sun, mud is hardened and wax melted; as after the same rain, tilled ground yields fruit but untilled ground thorns; so by the same long-suffering of God, some are hardened and others converted'. But this is no help to you at all. You maintain that all people are the same — all have 'free-will'. But it is election by God which makes a distinction between men. Without election all are free only to defy God. But you say there is no election. The result is that you are left with a helpless God and men and women are damned or saved without his knowledge. He simply sets his goodness before them. Then he can do no more than perhaps go off to a banquet! This is the best that human reason can do. But you have confused the issue by inventing two 'free-wills' — wax and clay; tilled and untilled. These illustrations are of no real use to you. They only make sense if we call the gospel the rain and the sun; the clay and the untilled ground the non-elect; and the wax and the tilled ground the elect. The non-elect are made worse by the gospel. The elect are made better by it.

You have invented this 'explanation' that Pharaoh hardened his own heart in the face of God's goodness because, you say, the idea that God who is good should have done it is absurd. Who says it is absurd? Only human reason is offended by it. Are we to judge God's action by human reason which is blind, deaf and godless? On these grounds, the whole Christian faith is absurd. As Paul says in I Corinthians 1:23, it is foolishness to the Greeks and a stumbling-block to the Jews that God should be man, a virgin's son, crucified and sitting at the Father's right hand. By human reason, it is certainly absurd to believe such things.

But in any case you haven't clarified the matter by asserting that man is responsible for hardening his own heart. You still have to explain how God can require 'free-will' to do impossible things. How can God charge 'free-will' with sin even though it can't do anything else? You appeal to reason. These things are equally absurd to human reason.

The fact remains that the exercise of all the 'free-will' in the world can never stop men hardening their hearts without the operation of the Holy Spirit.

You have said that God could not have made Pharaoh what he was because God saw that all he made was very good. But surely this is a reference to God's original creation before the Fall. From that time, all of us, including Pharaoh, have come from an ungodly and corrupt race. Even if these words are made to refer to God's works after the Fall, they refer to the way God sees things, not men. Many things are good in God's eyes that are bad in ours. For example — afflictions, sorrows, errors, hell and all God's best deeds are bad in the world's eyes. The gospel is best of all, but there is nothing that the world hates more.

Argument 4: God's use of human nature

Some people may want to know how God produces evil effects in us, hardening us, giving us up to our desires and causing us to go wrong. We ought to be content with what the Bible tells us.

My answer is that apart from electing grace, God deals with men according to their nature. Because their nature is evil and perverted, when God spurs them to action, their action is evil and perverted. Imagine a man riding a horse with only two or three good legs. His riding corresponds to what his horse is. The horse goes badly, but what can the rider do? He is riding this horse in company with sound horses; though the rest go well, his horse is bound to go badly, unless it is healed.

So you see, when God does things by evil men, evil things happen. But God himself cannot do evil. God is sovereign. Ungodly man is a creature of God and subject to God's control. God doesn't suspend his sovereignty because of man's evil. Ungodly man cannot alter his condition. As a result, man cannot help sinning and going astray continually, unless and until he is put right by the Spirit of God.

Argument 5: God's method of hardening man

Ungodly men are not concerned to please God. They're only interested in pleasing themselves. They hate and fight against anything that prevents them enjoying their selfish desires. This is especially so when ungodly men are confronted with the gospel. In the gospel, God cuts across their twisted desires and man-centred confidence, so that they become bitter and hard against God and his word.

God does not create new evil in men's hearts. He uses the evil that is already there for his own good and wise purposes. In II Samuel 16:10 David spoke of Shimei: 'Let him curse, for God has bidden him to curse'. But God had not issued a command that Shimei should curse David. Rather, God's sovereign action ensured that Shimei's already evil will would do what was natural to it at that moment and in the place that God intended.

Argument 6: God's hardening of Pharaoh's heart

With these things in mind, we come back to the case of Pharaoh. God did not change Pharaoh's nature by his Holy Spirit. Pharaoh's will remained ungodly and evil. He was full of his own greatness and power. So when God presented him with something that offended and irritated him, he could not help reacting in an evil way. He grew increasingly obstinate and refused to listen to reason.

The words of scripture must be understood according to their plain meaning. When God says: 'I will harden the heart of Pharaoh', he is saying: 'I will cause the heart of Pharaoh to be hardened'. God, with full certainty, knew and, with full certainty, declared that Pharaoh should be hardened. God knew with equal certainty that Pharaoh could not stop God's actions toward him. And God knew that as a result, Pharaoh would certainly grow worse. An evil will can only will to do evil. Even when God brings some good — such as the gospel — to bear on it, an evil will can only get worse. It becomes hardened.

Why doesn't God stop putting on pressure that will surely produce bad results? This is to ask God to stop being God. We can't really imagine that God will stop doing good just because the ungodly will react badly.

Why doesn't God alter the evil wills of people like Pharaoh? This question touches God's secret will, where his ways are past finding out (Romans 11:33). If anyone who is bound by human reason is offended by this, so be it. Grumbling will change nothing and God's elect will still hold fast. We might as well ask why God let Adam fall! We must not try to lay down rules for God. What God does is not right because we approve it but because God wills it. The only alternative is to set up another creator over God!

Let us return to the text. You ignore the plain meaning of the text because you don't like it and then put an 'explanation' of your own on it. But we must always examine a text in its context to discover the author's aim and purpose. The plain meaning is that God would harden Pharaoh's heart by means of the plagues. But you say it would be by means of God's longsuffering and by not immediately punishing Pharaoh. Yet look at the context. God had patiently waited for a long time while Pharaoh was inflicting great hardship on the Children of Israel. Clearly when God said he would harden Pharaoh's heart, he intended something different — a change from his longsuffering, not a

69

continuation of it. We know why there was a difference. God was intending to release his people from Egypt. He intended to give his people added reasons for confidence in him. Pharaoh's resistance would call forth more plagues and each new plague would demonstrate the power of God. Not only so, after each plague Moses records that 'Pharaoh's heart was hardened, as the Lord said'. Here was further strengthening for the Israelites' faith in God.

You want Pharaoh to have a will that is free to submit or to rebel, so you insist that the text means that Pharaoh hardened his own heart rather than that God did it. But see what that would mean. God would have been dependent on Pharaoh's 'free-will' and he could not have told Moses and his people in advance what would happen. But as it is, God hardened Pharaoh's heart. He moved Pharaoh to act and Pharaoh could do no other than act in harmony with his own nature. So we see that this passage cannot be made to support 'free-will' but only to argue forcefully against it.

Argument 7:   Erasmus' treatment of Romans 9:15–33

You are terribly tormented by this passage. You are determined to hold on to 'free-will' at all costs, so you say all kinds of contradictory things, especially about God's foreknowledge. Let us be quite clear about this. For example, God foreknew that Judas would be a traitor. Therefore, Judas had to be a traitor. Judas had no power to act differently. Of course, Judas acted freely and willingly in harmony with his nature. God knew in advance how Judas was bound to act and God brought the action into play when he decided to.

It is no use you talking about man's so-called

foreknowledge, because it falls a long way short of God's. We know, for example, that an eclipse is going to happen. But it does not happen because we forecast it. When God forecasts something, however, it happens because he forecasts it. If you don't accept this, then you undermine all God's promises and threatenings. You deny God himself.

In one place you have the sound sense to admit that Paul teaches that God wills what he foreknows, so it must happen. But then you spoil it by saying you find this difficult. You then try to escape by saying that Paul does not explain the point but merely rebukes the one arguing with him (Romans 9:20). This is no way to handle the sacred text. A glance at the passage will show that Paul does explain the matter. In fact, there would have been no reason for the rebuke if there were not people arguing against his explanation. Paul quotes Exodus 33:19: 'And the Lord said, "I will cause all my goodness to pass in front of you, and I will proclaim my name, the LORD, in your presence. I will have mercy on whom I will have mercy and I will have compassion on whom I will have compassion".' Then Paul explains that God's actions either of mercy or of hardening do not depend at all on man's will but only on God himself. Paul makes clear that God's foreknowledge guarantees the actions men take. Of course, if we try to prove both God's foreknowledge and man's 'free-will' together we do have problems — like trying to prove that the same number is both nine and ten!

Paul's rebuke is for those who object to the idea that they have no 'free-will' and that all things depend on the will of God alone. This is the place at which to adore the majesty of God in its awe-inspiring, wonderful, amazing judgments and to say: 'Your will be done, on earth as it is in heaven' (Matthew 6:10).

71

Argument 8: Natural reason must admit the sovereignty of God's will

Natural reason must admit that 'God' would be a very weak and pathetic deity if his foreknowledge was unreliable and could be contradicted by events. Of course, men will object to the thought that God, who is good, should abandon, harden and condemn them as though he delighted in their sins and eternal torment. I have stumbled at this myself more than once, down to the deepest pit of despair, so that I wished I had never been made a man. (That was before I knew how health-giving that despair was and how close to grace). This is why men have tried to find 'explanations' and have their own reasoning before what is plainly taught in God's Word.

But even though the reasoning of unbelief is offended, it would be forced to admit the sovereignty of God's will even if there were no Bible, for two things are written into the consciences of men — that God is sovereign and that he foreknows all things without exception or mistake.

Argument 9: Romans 9:15—33, continued

In Romans 9:20, 21 Paul says men are like clay and God is like a potter. Nothing could be clearer than that Paul's whole purpose is to deny 'free-will' in man. Paul's whole case in this epistle is that if there is power in man to save himself, grace is useless. And in chapter 11:20—23 when Paul is showing that many Gentiles would be saved, he credits this, not to their 'free-will' but to God's action — 'grafting them in'.

Argument 10: God's sovereignty and 'free-will' cannot live together

Here is an example of your reasoning. You say: 'With regard to the unbreakable foreknowledge of God, Judas was bound to become a traitor; even so, Judas was able to change his will'. Do you realise what you are saying? If you are right, Judas had the power to change God's foreknowledge and make it unreliable. You don't deal with the problem, however. You are like a captain who leads his army into the battle and then abandons it when his help is most needed! You start talking about something else — whether man's will is disturbed by God's sovereignty. I ask one question. You answer another! But I will not let you off the hook so easily. You must face your own dilemma. How can these two things agree? 'Judas can will not to betray' and 'Judas must necessarily will to betray'. Are they not directly opposed and contradictory?

Argument 11: Erasmus' treatment of Malachi 1:2—3

We must now turn to the second of the two texts you allow as possibly supporting my position on 'free-will', although you actually deny that it does. What is your argument? In Genesis 25:23 it says: 'the elder shall serve the younger'. Your 'explanation' goes like this: 'Rightly understood, it does not bear on man's salvation; for God may will that a man should be a servant and a pauper, without his being rejected from eternal salvation'.

What a slippery mind you have in trying to escape from the truth! But you cannot escape. Think of Paul's use of this text in Romans 9:12—13. Is Paul misusing scripture while he lays the foundation of Christian doctrine? Surely not! Jerome dares to say: 'Things have a force in Paul which they do not possess in their original context'. Jerome can say that, but that does not prove it. People like Jerome neither understand Paul nor the passages he quotes. I cannot agree that Genesis 25:21—23 refers only to one person serving another, but let us assume for the moment that it does We can still see that Paul quotes it correctly to prove that there was no merit in either Jacob or Esau. Paul is discussing whether they attained what was spoken of them by the merits of 'free-will' and he proves that they did not. All was determined before either of them was born.

Paul's comments on Genesis 25:23 are not to be taken to mean merely a lowly service. They do have a bearing on eternal salvation. Jacob was one of God's people. The promise to him included all that belongs to God's people — the blessing, the Word, the Spirit, the promise of Christ and his eternal kingdom. This is confirmed in Genesis 27:27 onwards. So our reply to Jerome is that all the passages quoted by the apostles have more force in their original context than they have in his writings!

As for the passage from Malachi 1:2—3 which Paul also quotes, it reads: ' "I have loved you' says the Lord. But you ask, "How have you loved us?" "Was not Esau Jacob's brother?" the Lord says. "Yet I have loved Jacob, but Esau I have hated, and I have turned his mountains into a wasteland and left his inheritance to the desert jackals".' You, Erasmus, have three ways of trying to escape the plain meaning of these words.

Your first is that we cannot take this literally because God's love and hate differ from man's, having no trace of human passions in them. Now we all know that God's love and hate do not involve human passions but the question we are facing demands that we ask not *how* God loves or hates but *why* God loves or hates. But because you want to divert attention to *how* God loves or hates, let us for a moment see if this helps your case. It does not. God's love and hate are not subject to change as ours are. In God, they are eternal and unchangeable. They were fixed before 'free-will' was ever possible, so we see that God's love or hate don't wait for man's response. This is even clearer when we ask *why* God hates or loves. What could possibly have made God love Jacob or hate Esau? Certainly nothing they did, because God's attitude to them was settled and declared before they were even born. There was not much exercise of 'free-will' at that stage!

Your second attempt to escape the plain meaning of the words is this: you say that Malachi does not seem to be speaking of the hatred by which we are eternally condemned. You suggest that Malachi is only speaking of troubles experienced on earth. Once again, this is a slanderous suggestion that Paul is using the scriptures wrongly. Again, let us see if the attempt to escape the plain meaning of the words helps your case. Surely, Paul's point in these verses is to emphasise the complete absence of merit or the exercise of 'free-will'. Even if Paul is only dealing with things experienced on earth, he is still using a proper illustration in Jacob and Esau. In any case, it is false to suggest that Malachi only refers to things experienced on earth. The context of the passage shows that his purpose is to rebuke the people of Israel because they did not respond to God's love to them. God's love to them meant more than earthly blessings, for the passage shows that our God is the God of all things. He's not going to be Israel's God who is content to have their half-hearted worship with half a shoulder or a lame leg (Malachi 1:13) from a sick animal! The true worship of God is to be with their whole heart and strength, for he is God both here and hereafter, in all matters, on all occasions, at all times and in all they do.

Your third attempt to avoid the plain meaning of Malachi 1:2—3 is to say that Malachi means God loves some Jews and hates other Jews. You think this opens the way for unbelief by some Jews by which they deserve to be cut off. And you think your 'interpretation' opens the way for the faith of other Jews by which they deserve to be grafted in again.

You don't know what you're talking about! I know very well that men are cut off by unbelief and grafted in by faith and that they must be encouraged and urged to believe. But this has nothing whatever to do with believing or not believing by the power of 'free-will'.

Argument 12: The potter and the clay

The third text you say could possibly support my position is Isaiah 45:9: 'Woe to him who quarrels with his maker; to him who is but a potsherd among the potsherds on the ground. Does the clay say to the potter, "What are you making?".' Also, Jeremiah 18:6: 'Like clay in the hand of the potter so are you in my hand, O house of Israel'. Clearly these texts do support my case but you try to evade their force by making the potter's work refer to our experiences in this life. You suggest that when Paul uses these texts in Romans 9 he adds to their supposed original meaning by making them refer to personal election. This is to malign Paul. Then you add to your confusion by referring to II Timothy 2:20—21: 'In a large house there are articles not only of gold and silver, but also of wood and clay; some are for noble purposes and some for ignoble. If a man cleanses himself from the latter, he will be an instrument for noble purposes, made holy, useful to the Master and prepared to do any good work'. You say that Paul here is writing about the same theme as in Isaiah 45:9; Jeremiah 18:6 and Romans 9. You ridicule the idea of an earthenware pot purifying itself. Yet you say Paul does command the pot to do so and prove to your own satisfaction that the pot must therefore represent men with 'free-will'.

My answer in fact is that Paul in II Timothy 2:20—21 is not referring to the same theme as in the other texts. He is using a homely picture to illustrate a different theme altogether — the believer's personal godliness. Furthermore, it is not the pots, but believers, who are commanded to act. They must cleanse themselves from all that dishonours God. As for the pots, some are honourable and some are not, and it is their master, not the articles themselves, who decides their individual use.

Argument 13: The righteousness of God

Now you resort to human reasoning. You cannot accept God's right to cast the wicked into eternal fire. This is unreasonable, you suggest, because God made them as they are. So the truth is out! You put yourself in the shoes of the grumblers whom Paul is quoting in Romans 9:19: 'Why does God still blame us? For who resists his will?' So human reasoning demands that God should act according to man's ideas of what is right and what is wrong. The Majesty that created all things must submit to his own creation! Rules must be laid down that God can only condemn those who deserve it *by our reckoning*! When God saves those who deserve otherwise, no-one complains. But when God condemns them, there is a great protest. The wickedness of the human heart is shown here. When men reason like this, they are failing to praise God as God. They rob God of his sovereign right. We shall never understand how a just God can save ungodly men until we reach heaven. So how shall we understand how a just God can condemn the ungodly? Yet faith will continue to believe it is so, till the Son of man shall be revealed.

Argument 14: Paul credits the salvation of man to God alone

There are no contradictions in the scriptures unless you insist on your 'explanations'. It is then that confusion arises. For example, there is no contradiction between 'If a man cleanses himself' (II Timothy 2:20—21) and 'God works all . . .' (I Corinthians 12:6). The first of these simply lays down what man should do. This does not mean he has the ability to do it by 'free-will', apart from grace. I know you are convinced that when a command is given it implies an ability to obey. But that is nonsense. The second text clearly states that all things are the work of God. There is no contradiction. Paul is consistent in all his teaching that the salvation of man is by the power of God alone.

Chapter Four

Luther's comments on Erasmus' treatment of texts that deny 'free-will'

At last we can come to the point where you deal with the text I have used to prove 'free-will' is false.

Argument 1: Genesis 6:3 'My Spirit shall not always remain in man seeing he is flesh' (Luther)

First of all you argue that 'flesh' here means human weakness. But the meaning here is the same as in I Corinthians 3:1—3 where Paul calls the Corinthians 'carnal' or 'worldly'. Paul is not referring to weakness, but to corruption. Moses is referring to men who were marrying out of mere lust and who were filling the earth with violence, to the extent that the Spirit of God could not continue with them. You will notice that in the scriptures wherever 'flesh' is contrasted with 'spirit' it means all that is opposed to the Spirit of God. Only when 'flesh' is used on its own does it refer to the physical body. So the passage means: 'My Spirit, which is in Noah and other holy men, rebukes the ungodly through the word that these men preach and through their godly lives. But it is in vain, for the ungodly are blinded and hardened by the flesh and grow worse the more they are judged'. This always happens and it is obvious that if men go from worse to worse even while the Spirit is working among them, they must be completely helpless without the Spirit. 'Free-will' can do nothing except sin.

Next you tell us that the text does not refer to all men but only to those who lived at the time. This will not do, for Christ said of all men: 'Flesh gives birth to flesh' (John 3:6). And he underlined the seriousness of this condition by saying: 'Unless a man is born again he cannot see the kingdom of God' (John 3:3).

Then you say that the text does not mean the judgment of God but his mercy. But all you have to do is to read what goes before and after the text. There can be no doubt that they are the words of an angry God. So the text stands in opposition to 'free-will'. It shows there is no power in man to do good but only to merit the judgment of God.

Argument 2:   Genesis 8:21 'Every inclination of (man's) heart is evil from childhood'. See also Genesis 6:5 'Every inclination of the thoughts of (man's) heart was only evil all the time'

You seek to avoid the plain meaning of this text by saying that there is a likelihood of evil in most people but this does not rob them of their freedom of will.

But God speaks here of *all* men, not merely of *most*. After the flood, God is saying that he will no longer treat men as they deserve. If he did, no-one would be saved. Both before and after the flood, God declares all men to be evil, not just some of them. You seem to treat sin in man very lightly, as something that can easily be corrected. But the passage says that all the energy of man's will is to do evil. Why don't you consult the Hebrew? Moses actually says: 'Every inclination of the thoughts of his heart was only evil all the time' (Genesis 6:5). This is no mere likelihood of evil. God says that nothing but evil is thought of or imagined by man throughout his life. But you may reply: 'Why then does God allow time for repentance if it is not in man's power to repent?' The answer, as we have frequently said, is that God's commands by no means imply our ability to obey. God tells us our duty, not to prove that we can do it but to humble us to admit that we can't!

Argument 3:   Isaiah 40:1–2 'Comfort, comfort my people, says your God. Speak tenderly to Jerusalem and proclaim to her that her hard service has been completed, that her sin has been paid for, that she has received from the Lord's hand double for all her sins'

This passage means that God's pardon is given to those totally unable to earn it or to merit it in any way. You, however, disagree. You say it means God's vengeance on our sins, not his grace. But when I turn to the New Testament, I find that this passage speaks of God's pardon for sin proclaimed by the gospel! Let us look at the text.

I presume the word 'comfort' doesn't mean the execution of God's judgment! Then it says: 'speak tenderly to Jerusalem'. This means: 'speak to the heart' of Jerusalem, speak words of love — sweet, kind words. Then, 'hard service' means the terrible burden of struggling to earn pardon by obedience to the law (see

Acts 15:7—10). That hard service is ended because of God's free pardon. The people have 'received double' from the Lord's hand, which means both remission of sin and release from the terrible burden of the law. And this remission and release is from 'all her sin', which means that she (the people) was all sin and nothing but sin. Grace is not the reward of the attempts of 'free-will'. Grace is given in the face of sins and all they deserve.

Argument 4:   Isaiah 40:6—7 'All flesh is as grass and all the glory of it as the flower of grass: the grass is withered, the flower of grass is fallen: because the Spirit of the Lord hath blown upon it' (Luther)

You say that 'spirit' in the text means anger, and that 'flesh' is the weakness of man that has no power against God. But really, has the anger of God nothing else to wither, that it has to pick on man's unhappy weakness? Should it not rather raise it up?

Then you say that the 'flower of grass' represents the glory that comes from prosperity in material things. But this cannot be right. The Jews gloried in their temple, in circumcision and in sacrifices. The Greeks gloried in their wisdom. It is therefore the so-called righteousness of works and human wisdom that is scattered by God's Spirit blowing on it. This is confirmed by Isaiah's reference to 'all flesh'. Only some people glory in material prosperity but all men naturally glory in human deeds and wisdom.

At this point it is important to take notice of John 3:6: 'Flesh gives birth to flesh but the Spirit gives birth to spirit'. This text clearly shows that whatever is not born of God's Spirit is flesh. This does not mean that only a part, a large part, of natural man is flesh. It certainly does not mean that the most excellent thing in man is flesh. It clearly means that all men without the Spirit of God are 'flesh' and therefore subject to God's judgment.

You think that this is not true. You think there are some men who would rather die a thousand deaths than commit a vile act, although no-one else knew of it and God would pardon it. But you are still looking at outward acts. You must look at the heart. Even if such people exist, their behaviour brings glory to themselves because apart from the Spirit they have no desire to glorify God by their actions.

You also ask if all that is called 'flesh' must of necessity be called ungodly. I answer, Yes; a man is ungodly if he is without the Spirit of God. Scripture says that the Spirit is given to justify the ungodly. Jesus said that what is born of the flesh cannot see the kingdom of God. There is no middle ground between the kingdom of God and the kingdom of Satan. If a man is not in God's kingdom, he must be in Satan's.

Then you ask: 'How can I teach that man is nothing but flesh even when he is born of the Spirit?' Where did you dream up such a thing? I draw a clear-cut distinction between 'flesh' and 'Spirit'. A man who is not born of the Spirit is flesh. A man who is born of the Spirit, is Spirit — except for those elements of the flesh that remain to trouble him.

Argument 5: Jeremiah 10:23 'I know, O Lord, that a man's life is not his own; it is not for man to direct his steps'

Here again you twist the plain meaning of the text. You

say that it means that God, not man, causes events to have a happy outcome and that it is nothing to do with 'free-will'. But do Jeremiah's words need any explanation? Surely Jeremiah simply means that the stubbornness of the people in refusing God's Word convinced him that man is unable to do good by his own power.

But even suppose your idea is right – what good does it do? If a man cannot make natural events turn out happily, how can he do anything about his spiritual destiny?

You argue that many people realise their need for God's grace to live rightly and they pursue this by praying daily for God's help. You say that by doing this they use human effort. But you are not proving the power of 'free-will'. Who will ask for God's help except those in whom God's Spirit dwells? He who prays, does so by the Spirit (Romans 8:26–27).

Argument 6: Proverbs 16:1 'To man belong the plans of the heart, but the Lord governs the tongue' (Luther)

You want this once again to refer to the ordinary events of life. Once again I reply that even if you are right, it makes even more unlikely our deciding our spiritual destiny for ourselves. And the fact that everything in the future is decided by God should produce a fear of God within us.

You link this text with two more from the book of Proverbs: Proverbs 16:4 – 'The Lord has made all things for himself, yes, even the wicked for the day of evil' (Luther). You do well to point out that this does not mean that God made any creature evil. Bravo! I never said he did!

Proverbs 21:1 — 'The king's heart is in the hand of the Lord; he inclines it wherever he pleases' (Luther). You say that the word 'incline' does not mean 'compel'. You say that the king is inclined to evil by God allowing him to give way to his passions. But it doesn't matter whether you think of God's permission, or of God's inclination, it is still true that nothing happens apart from the will and work of God. The text refers to one man — the king. If it is true of one man, it is true of all.

Argument 7:   John 15:5 'I am the vine; you are the branches. If a man remains in me and I in him, he will bear much fruit; apart from me you can do nothing'

This was the text I said no-one could escape from, but you take hold of the little word 'nothing' and cut its throat! You say it can mean 'nothing perfectly' and so reads, 'apart from me you can do nothing perfectly'. The question is not whether it *can* mean that, but whether it *does* mean that. You say it means that without Christ we can do a 'little imperfect something'. So I suppose when John 1:3 says: 'without him nothing was made', it means 'without him a little imperfect something was made'. What stupidity! It is highly dangerous to treat scripture like this. And it is no way to reach the consciences of men. Let it be settled that 'nothing' here means 'nothing'.

Under Satan's rule, the human will is no longer free, nor in its own power, but is the slave of sin and Satan and can only will what its prince has willed. You ignore what follows in the text: 'If anyone does not remain in me, he is like a branch that is thrown away and withers; such branches are picked up, thrown into the fire and burned' (verse 6). Man outside of Christ is totally unacceptable to God and is thrown into the fire.

I can't understand why you also quote I Corinthians 13:2 to support your case. 'If I have the gift of prophecy and can fathom all mysteries and all knowledge, and if I have a faith that can move mountains, but have not love, I am nothing'. If anyone is without love, he is in a true sense nothing before God, for this love is a gift of grace. So it comes to this: 'nothing' means *nothing*, and nothing can alter that! Apart from grace a man can do nothing. 'Free-will' can do nothing and is nothing.

Argument 8: Man's co-operation with God does not prove 'free-will'

You use a number of illustrations that describe man's co-operation with God's operations. For example, 'the farmer gathers the harvest but God gave it'. Of course I am aware of man's co-operation with God but this proves nothing about 'free-will'. God is omnipotent. He is in total control of all that he alone created. And this includes the ungodly, who, together with those whom God has justified and brought into his kingdom, co-operate with God in this world. All men must follow and obey what God intends them to do.

Man made no contribution to his own creation. And, having been created, man makes no contribution to his continuing as God's creation. Both his creation and his continuation are entirely the responsibility of the sovereign power and goodness of God, who creates and preserves us without any help from us.

Man, before he is renewed into the new creation of the Spirit's kingdom, contributes nothing to prepare himself for that new creation and kingdom. Similarly, when he is created anew, he contributes nothing towards being kept in that kingdom. The Spirit alone both regenerates and preserves us when regenerate, without any help from us. As James says: 'He chose to give us birth through the word of truth, that we might be a kind of firstfruits of all he created' (James 1:18). (James is speaking of the renewed creation). But God does not regenerate us without us being aware of it, for he re-creates us and preserves us for this very purpose, that we might co-operate with him.

And what is credited to 'free-will' in all this? What is left to it? Nothing! Absolutely nothing!

Conclusion

In this controversy, I don't want to generate more heat than light. But if I have argued somewhat strongly, I acknowledge my fault, if it is a fault. But no; I have an assurance that this testimony of mine is carried to the world all the more urgently in the cause of God. May God confirm this testimony in the last day! Who would then be happier than I — approved by the testimony of others of having maintained the cause of truth, not lazily, nor deceitfully, but with vigour enough and to spare!

If I seem too bitter against you, I ask you to pardon me. I do not act so out of ill-will; but I was concerned that by the weight of your name you were damaging the cause of Christ. And who can always so govern his pen as not on occasion to show warmth? Even you often throw flaming darts against me. But these things have no bearing on the debate, and we who engage in it must freely pardon each other for them; for we are all but men and there is nothing in us that is not characteristic of mankind. May the Lord, whose cause this is, open your eyes and help you to glorify him. Amen.

Postscript:

The later history of the controversy and its importance today.

What is the 20th century reader to make of the controversy which lies behind Luther's book 'Bondage of the Will'? As you have read this abridged and simplified version, you must have been impressed by his great ability in an argument. But what really ought to concern us is whether or not his case is a scriptural one. If what he wrote is the teaching of God's Word, we need to take notice of it today.

Some people will simply conclude that what Luther wrote is now called Calvinism and will therefore pass it by. The Lutheran church in modern times seems to have done just that and there's no doubt that many evangelical Christians of today will do exactly the same thing.

If we look at the time of the Reformation, it is clear that the Protestant leaders — Luther, Zwingli, Calvin, Bucer, Beza, Melancthon, John Knox, etc. — all agreed that man is, by nature, unable to do anything towards his salvation and that God is absolutely sovereign in grace. The reformers may have differed about some other things but they all agreed about this. It would be true to say that this was really the basic doctrine of the Reformation. Very often the doctrine of justification by faith is thought to be the central truth in reformation theology. But the reformers, in returning to the teaching of the Apostle Paul, emphasised that a sinner's salvation in its entirety is by the free grace of God alone. The doctrine of justification by faith is important because it safeguards the principle that man is a helpless sinner, saved only by God's grace. But the central truth of the Reformation was the truth that God's grace is sovereign and free.

Opposition to the stand taken by the reformers never completely stopped. It flared up strongly in the Arminian heresy which denied that man is totally helpless and suggested that salvation really rests on something we do for ourselves. These things were taught by a man called Van Harmen (Arminius) who became professor of theology at Leyden University in the Netherlands in 1603. In 1618 an international synod met at Dortrecht (Dort) and sat for six months. The teachings of Arminius and his followers were rejected and denounced.

Arminianism did not die with the Synod of Dort. It is still alive and active. John Wesley popularised it and it is still popular. What Arminian teaching does is divide up the salvation of sinners between God and the sinners themselves. Part of salvation is said to be God's work and part the sinners are said to do for themselves. The teaching of the Bible, on which the reformers agreed, gives God all the credit in our salvation. Salvation depends on the sovereign grace of God, the perfect and complete work of Christ, and the effective and all-powerful work of the Holy Spirit. God receives all the glory: 'salvation is of the Lord'.

Arminianism is very close to the teaching of Rome

about salvation, for both teach that God is unable to save a sinner without his co-operation! (If the sinner's co-operation is essential, how would Saul of Tarsus ever have been saved?) Arminian teaching is a denial and a rejection of New Testament Christianity in favour of a religion of works. To rely on yourself for faith is no different from relying on yourself for works. The one is as non-Christian as the other.

The book you have just read is about a vital matter. What Luther fought for still needs fighting for. What the reformers stood for still needs standing for. Luther, and the other reformers, taught a salvation by grace, as clearly revealed in God's Word. There is no more important matter than that today. What Luther wrote is still needed today! The Word of God never goes out of date and God still speaks to men today as he has always done.

GREAT CHRISTIAN CLASSICS

No. 1 Life by His Death!

An easier-to-read and abridged version of the classic "The Death of Death in the Death of Christ" by John Owen, first published in 1647.

Paperback, 100 pages, £1.50

". . . a brilliant abridgement of that wonderful book. The whole church of Christ stands in debt to John Appleby for undertaking this work. It will open the door into Owen's volume for countless believers who might otherwise miss its treasures." Evangelical Times.

No. 2 God Willing

An easier-to-read and abridged version of the classic "Divine Conduct or the Mystery of Providence" by John Flavel, first published in 1677.

Paperback, 78 pages, £1.50

No. 3 Biblical Christianity

An easier-to-read and abridged version of the classic "Institutes of the Christian Religion" by John Calvin, first published in 1536.

John Calvin's "Institutes of the Christian Religion" is perhaps the finest summary of Christian truth since the apostles, yet its very size and comprehensiveness has been a stumbling block to many. Biblical Christianity, written as an easier-to-read and abridged version, offers an ideal introduction to a work with which every Christian should be familiar.

Paperback, 125 pages, £1.95

No. 4 By God's Grace Alone

An easier-to-read and abridged version of the classic "The Reign of Grace" by Abraham Booth, first published in 1768.

Paperback, 80 pages, £1.35

GRACE GATEWAY BOOKS

Introductions to Great Christian Writings

1. WHO IS IN CONTROL?

An easy-to-read version of the substance of "The Sovereignty of God" by A. W. Pink, prepared by Roger Devenish.

Paperback, 60 pages, £1.20.

2. INTO LIFE

An easy-to-read version of the substance of "The Rise and Progress of Religion in the Soul" by Philip Doddridge, prepared by Roger Devenish.

Paperback, 60 pages, £1.20.